D0777356

Library of Congress Cataloging in Publication Data

Main entry under title:

Owls.

1. Owls — Quotations, maxims, etc. 2. Owls in art.
I. Hughes, Lynn.
PN6084.O9309   820'.8'036   79-411
ISBN 0-89480-109-0

Book design: Nick Thirkell
Picture research: Irene Reed

Workman Publishing
1 West 39 Street
New York, New York 10018

Manufactured in the United States of America
First printing September 1979
10 9 8 7 6 5 4 3 2

Sweet Suffolk owl, so trimly dight
With feathers like a lady bright,
Thou sing'st alone, sitting by night,
   Te whit, te whoo.
The note that forth so freely rolls
With shrill command the mouse controls
And sings a dirge for dying souls,
   Te whit, te whoo.

THOMAS VATOUR
SWEET SUFFOLK OWL

A wise old owl sat in an oak,
The more he saw the less he spoke,
The less he spoke the more he heard,
Why can't we all be like that wise old bird.

ANON
PUNCH *1875*

Save that from yonder ivy-mantled tow'r,
The mopeing owl does to the moon complain
Of such, as wandering near her sacred bow'r,
Molest her ancient solitary reign.

THOMAS GRAY
ELEGY WRITTEN IN A COUNTRY CHURCHYARD

On eves of cold, when slow coal fires,
rooted in basements, burn and branch,
brushing with smoke the city air;
When quartered moons pale in the sky,
and neons glow along the dark
like deadly nightshade on a briar;
Above the muffled traffic then
I hear the owl, and at his note
I shudder in my private chair.
For like an augur he has come
to roost among our crumbling walls,
his blooded talons sheathed in fur.
Some secret lure of time it seems
has called him from his country wastes
to hunt a newer wasteland here.
And where the candelabra swung
bright with the dancers' thousand eyes,
now his black, hooded pupils stare,
And where the silk-shoed lovers ran
with dust of diamonds in their hair,
he opens now his silent wing,
And, like a stroke of doom, drops down,
and swoops across the empty hall,
and plucks a quick mouse off the stair . . .

LAURIE LEE
TOWN OWL

11

I know how cruelly you attack
Small birds who cannot fight you back;
At every opportunity
You peck and tear them wantonly.
And that is why all birds detest you,
Why when they find you they molest you,
Screeching and crying as they chase
And mob you till you leave the place.
Even the tiniest of the tits
Would gladly tear you into bits!
For you are loathsome through and through
And wholly hateful to the view:
Your neck is thin, your body squat,
Your head much bigger than the lot.
Your eyes are black as coal, and broad,
As if they had been daubed with woad.
You glare as if you'd gorge on such
As come within your talons' clutch.
Your beak is hooked and sharp and strong.
A buckled awl, its shape gone wrong.
With it you gabble loud and long,
And that is what you call your song.

ANON
THE OWL AND THE NIGHTINGALE

We have had, ever since I can remember, a pair of white owls that constantly breed under the eaves of this church. During their season of breeding, which lasts the summer through, about an hour before sunset (for then the mice begin to run) these birds sally forth in quest of prey, and hunt all round the hedges of meadows and small inclosures for them, which seem to be their only food. In this irregular country we can stand on an eminence and see them beat the fields over like a setting-dog, and often drop down in the grass or corn. I have minuted these birds with my watch for an hour together, and have found that they return to their nest, the one or the other of them, about once in five minutes. But a piece of address, which they show when they return loaded, should not, I think, be passed over in silence. As they take their prey with their claws, so they carry it in their claws to their nest; but, as the feet are necessary in their ascent under the tiles, they constantly perch first on the roof of the chancel, and shift the mouse from their claws to their bill, that their feet may be at liberty to take hold of the plate on the wall as they are rising under the eaves.

GILBERT WHITE
NATURAL HISTORY OF SELBORNE

The truth of the matter, the truth of the
 matter—
As one who supplies us with hats is a Hatter,
As one who is known for his growls is a
 Growler—
My Grandpa traps owls, yes, my grandpa's an
 Owler.
'Owls are such sages,' he says, 'I surmise
Listening to owls could make the world wise.'
Nightlong his house is shaken with hoots,
And he wakes to owls in his socks and his
 boots.
Owls, owls, nothing but owls,
The most fantastical of fowls:
White owls from the Arctic, black owls from
 the Tropic.
Some are far-sighted, others myopic.
There are owls on his picture frames, owls on
 his chairs,
Owls in dozens ranked on his stairs.
Eyes, eyes, rows of their eyes.
Some are big as collie dogs, some are thumb-
 size.

TED HUGHES
MY GRANDPA

The Owl and the Pussy-Cat went to sea
In a beautiful pea-green boat,
They took some honey, and plenty of money,
Wrapped up in a five-pound note.
The Owl looked up to the Stars above
And sang to a small guitar,
'O lovely Pussy! O Pussy, my love,
What a beautiful Pussy you are.'

EDWARD LEAR
THE OWL AND THE PUSSY-CAT

God's silent searching flight:
When my Lord's head is filled with dew, and
   all
His locks are wet with the clear drops of night;
   His still soft call;
His knocking time; the soul's dumb watch,
When spirits their fair kindred catch.

HENRY VAUGHAN
THE NIGHT

Forth from his dark and lonely hiding-place
(Portentous sight)! the owlet Atheism,
Sailing on obscene wings athwart the noon,
Drops his blue-fringed lids, and holds them
    close,
And hooting at the glorious sun in Heaven,
Cries out, "Where is it?"

COLERIDGE
FEARS IN SOLITUDE

Deeply regret inform your grace last night two black owls came and perched on battlements remained there through night hooting at dawn flew away none knows whither awaiting instructions. Jellings.

MAX BEERBOHM
ZULEIKA DOBSON

Downhill I came, hungry, and yet not starved;
Cold, yet had heat within me that was proof
Against the North wind; tired, yet so that rest
Had seemed the sweetest thing under a roof.

Then at the inn I had food, fire, and rest,
Knowing how hungry, cold, and tired was I.
All of the night was quite barred out except
An owl's cry, a most melancholy cry

Shaken out long and clear upon the hill,
No merry note, nor cause of merriment,
But one telling me plain what I escaped
And others could not, that night, as in I went.

And salted was my food, and my repose,
Salted and sobered, too, by the bird's voice
Speaking for all who lay under the stars,
Soldiers and poor, unable to rejoice.

EDWARD THOMAS
THE OWL

The owl's cry and her singing,
Her constant screech and laughter,
And the false notes from her throat.
Till dawning, mournful passion,
She keeps singing, mournful cry,
'Hoo-thee-hoo,' lively longing.
Full force, by Saint Anne's grandson,
She stirs up the curs of night.
She's a slut, two tuneless cries,
Thick head, persistent crying,
Broad forehead, berry-bellied,
Staring old mouse-hunting hag.
Dry her voice, her colour tin,
Loud gabble in the south wood,
O that song, roebuck's copses,
And her face, a meek maiden's,
And her shape, a ghostly bird.
Every bird, filthy outlaw,
Beats her; how strange she still lives.
Fool owl who croons to robbers,
Cursed be her tongue and her tune!
I have a song for scaring
The owl from my neighbourhood:
I'll set, waiting for winter,
A blaze by each ivied tree.

DAFYDD AP GWILYM
THE OWL

From Wye Cliff to Pont Faen. Miss Child in great force. She told me the adventures of the brown wood owl 'Ruth' which she took home from here last year. She wanted to call the owl 'Eve' but Mrs Bridge said it should be called 'Ruth'. She and her sister stranded in London at night went to London Bridge hotel (having missed the last train) with little money and no luggage except the owl in a basket. The owl hooted all night in spite of their putting it up the chimney, before the looking glass, under the bedclothes, and in a circle of lighted candles which they hoped it would mistake for the sun. The owl went on hooting, upset the basket, got out and flew about the room. The chambermaid almost frightened to death dared not come inside the door. Miss Child asked the waiter to get some mice for 'Ruth' but none could be got.

KILVERT'S DIARY
Tuesday, 8 February 1870

Only a hoot owl
Hollows, a grassblade blown in cupped hands,
    in the looted elms
And no green cocks or hens
Shout
Now on Sir John's hill. The heron, ankling
    the scaly
Lowlands of the waves,
Makes all the music; and I who hear the tune
    of the slow,
Wear-willow river, grave,
Before the lunge of the night, the notes on
    this time-shaken
Stone for the sake of the souls of the slain
    birds sailing.

DYLAN THOMAS
OVER SIR JOHN'S HILL

When icicles hang by the wall,
And Dick, the shepherd, blows his nail
And Tom bears logs into the hall,
And milk comes frozen home in pail,
When blood is nipp'd and ways be foul,
Then nightly sings the staring owl, Tu-who;
Tu-whit, tu-who—a merry note,
While greasy Joan doth keel the pot.

SHAKESPEARE
LOVE'S LABOUR'S LOST

THE brown owl sits in the ivy bush,
   And she looketh wondrous wise,
With a horny beak beneath her cowl,
   And a pair of large round eyes.

She sat all day on the selfsame spray,
   From sunrise till sunset;
And the dim, grey light it was all too bright
   For the owl to see in yet.

'Jenny Owlet, Jenny Owlet,' said a merry
   little bird,
   'They say you're wondrous wise;
But I don't think you see, though you're
   looking at *me*
   With your large, round, shining eyes.'

But night came soon, and the pale white moon
   Rolled high up in the skies;
And the great brown owl flew away in her
   cowl,
   With her large, round, shining eyes.

JANE EUPHEMIA BROWNE
THE GREAT BROWN OWL

I would fain know what man ever found a scritch-owl's nest and met with any of their eggs, considering that it is held for an uncouth and strange prodigy to have seen the bird itself. And what might be he that tried such conclusions and experiments, especially in the hair of his head.

The feet of a scritch owl burnt together with the herb Plumbago, is very good against serpents. But before I write further of this bird, I cannot pass over the vanity of Magicians which herein appeareth most evidently; for over and besides many other monstrous lies which they have devised, they give it out that if one do lay the heart of a scritch-owl on the left pap of a woman as she lies asleep, she will disclose and utter all the secrets of her heart; also, whosoever carry about them the same heart when they go to fight, shall be more hardy, and perform their devoir the better against their enemies.

PLINY
NATURAL HISTORY

Griffin sculp.

39

Here lies a tree which Owl (a bird)
Was fond of when it stood on end,
And Owl was talking to a friend
Called Me (in case you hadn't heard)
When something Oo occurred.

A. A. MILNE
THE HOUSE AT POOH CORNER

Lovely are the curves of the white owl
    sweeping
Wavy in the dusk lit by one large star.
Lone on the fir-branch, his rattle-note
    unvaried,
Brooding o'er the gloom, spins the brown
    eve-jar.
Darker grows the valley, more and more
    forgetting:
So were it with me if forgetting could be
    willed.
Tell the grassy hollow that holds the bubbling
    well-spring,
Tell it to forget the source that keeps it filled.

MEREDITH
LOVE IN THE VALLEY

Nyctimine now freed from day,
From sullen bush flies out to prey,
And does with ferret note proclaim
Th'arrival of th'usurping Dame.

JOSEPH COTTON
NIGHT QUATRAINS

The owl thinks all her young ones beauties.

THOS FULLER
GNOMOLOGIA

The boding Owl, that in despair
  Doth moan and shiver on warm nights—
Shall that bird prophesy for me
  The fall of Heaven's eternal lights?
When in the thistled field of Age
  I take my final walk on earth,
Still will I make that Owl's despair
  A thing to fill my heart with mirth.

W. H. DAVIES
THE OWL

To Lorna H. 1977   John Reits

They come as a boon and a blessing to men,
The Pickwick, the Owl, and the Waverley pen.

ANONYMOUS ADVERTISEMENT

It was the owl that shriek'd, the fatal bellman,
Which gives the stern'st good-night.

SHAKESPEARE
MACBETH

Picture acknowledgments

For permission to use copyrighted material we are indebted to the following:

André Deutsch for 'The Town Owl' by Laurie Lee taken from *My Many Coated Man;* Penguin Books Ltd for an extract from 'The Owl and the Nightingale' (translated by Brian Stone), Penguin Classics 1971 © Brian Stone 1971; The Bobbs-Merrill Company, Inc. for 'My Grandpa' by Ted Hughes taken from *Meet My Folks,* copyright © 1961, 1973 by Ted Hughes; Myfanwy Thomas for 'The Owl' by Edward Thomas taken from *The Collected Poems* by Edward Thomas, published by Faber & Faber; *Poetry Wales* for 'The Owl' by Dafydd ap Gwilym (translated by Joseph Clancy); Jonathan Cape Ltd and the estate of F.R. Fletcher for an extract from 'Kilvert's Diary' (edited by William Plomer); the Trustees for the Copyrights of the late Dylan Thomas for "Over Sir John's Hill" by Dylan Thomas taken from *The Collected Poems of Dylan Thomas,* published by J.M. Dent & Sons Ltd; E.P. Dutton for an extract from *The House at Pooh Corner* by A.A. Milne, illustrated by Ernest Shepard, copyright, 1928, by E.P. Dutton & Co, Inc, renewal copyright, 1956, by A.A. Milne; Jonathan Cape Ltd for 'The Owl' by W.H. Davies taken from *The Complete Poems of W.H. Davies.*

Author's acknowledgments and thanks to Judith Burnley, Sally Gainham and J.P. Ward.